WRITING AND STAGING

Adventure Plays

Charlotte Guillain

capstone

Edited by James Benefield
Designed by Philippa Jenkins
Original illustrations © Capstone Global Library Limited 2016
Picture research by Kelly Garvin
Production by Victoria Fitzgerald
Originated by Capstone Global Library Ltd
Printed and bound in China

19 18 17 16 15
10 9 8 7 6 5 4 3 2 1

Library of Congress Cataloging-in-Publication Data
Cataloging-in-publication data is available at the Library of Congress.
ISBN 978 1 4846 2770 9 (hardback)
ISBN 978 1 4846 2774 7 (paperback)
ISBN 978 1 4846 2777 8 (ebook PDF)

Acknowledgments
Photo credits: Alamy/Roger Bamber, 37; Capstone Press/Karon Dubke, cover, 21, 24, 25, 39, 40; Corbis: Franz-Marc Frei, 34, H. Lorren Au Jr/ZUMA Press, 29, Hill Street Studios/Blend Images, 6, Martin Schutt, 8, Peter M. Fisher, 28, 32 Robbie Jack, 10, 27, Rune Hellestad/Sygma, 9, Ryan Pyle, 41, Scott Moore, 14; Getty Images: Christopher Furlong, 18, George Karger, 15, Hill Street Studios/Blend Images, 42, John Elk III/Lonely Planet Images, 43; iStockphoto: Alina Solovyova-Vincent, 16, jonas unruh, 36, Susan Chiang, 22; Glow Images/J-C&D Prett/Photononstop, 30; Newscom: Alastair Muir/REX, 4, DDAA/ZOB WENN Photos, 20, Ma Ping Xinhua News Agency, 26, New Line Cinema/Scholastic Productions/Depth of Field/Ingeni/Album, 12, Warner Bros. 13; Shutterstock: Arogant, 31, Dmytro Vietrov, 23, GlebStock, 19, LiliGraphie, 33, Michael Dechev, 35, Narcis Parfenti, 5, Sean Pavone, 38.

Artistic elements: Shutterstock/3DDock.

We would like to thank Mike Gould for his invaluable advice for this book.

Every effort has been made to contact copyright holders of any material reproduced in this book. Any omissions will be rectified in subsequent printings if notice is given to the publisher.

All the Internet addresses (URLs) given in this book were valid at the time of going to press. However, due to the dynamic nature of the Internet, some addresses may have changed, or sites may have changed or ceased to exist since publication. While the author and publisher regret any inconvenience this may cause readers, no responsibility for any such changes can be accepted by either the author or the publisher.07486CTPS

CONTENTS

Some words are shown in bold,
like this. You can find out what they
mean by looking in the glossary.

STAGING AN ADVENTURE

Performing in a play is one of the ways people share stories with one another. Instead of reading a story in a book, audiences can watch an adventure unfold in front of them in a play, bringing the action, **tension**, and humor to life. People have been writing, performing, and watching plays for thousands of years because it is so enjoyable and powerful to share a story in this way.

People involved in staging a play

Most plays start with a **script**. A writer called a **playwright** creates the script, thinking about what works well on a stage. The script for a play is a different type of text than a novel, poem, or even a movie script, because the story should be designed to take place in a live performance. Although this means there are limits to what is possible in a play, it is also a very exciting way to tell an adventure story.

Peter Pan is a play full of magic and excitement.

The stage in many theaters faces the audience and has an arch over the top of it.

Plays that tell an adventure story are some of the most popular and exciting to watch. *Peter Pan* is a play by J. M. Barrie, which tells the story of a boy who can fly and who also does not grow up. He takes a girl named Wendy and her brothers to the island of Neverland, where they have many thrilling adventures.

A team of people is needed to stage a play. In addition to actors, many people are needed behind the scenes, including a **director**, a **set** designer, a costume designer, and people in charge of **props**, lighting, and sound. All these people have to work well together to stage a successful play. Plays can be performed in all kinds of places: in a professional theater, a community center, the school auditorium—even outdoors. Staging a play can be hard work, but it can also be extremely rewarding and fun for all those involved.

The parts of a play script

Play scripts look different than the other texts that tell stories. Most of the text in the script is **dialogue**—the words the actors speak. These words are also called the actors' **lines**. In a play script, the names of the characters who speak in a scene appear on the left-hand side. Their lines will appear after their names. For example:

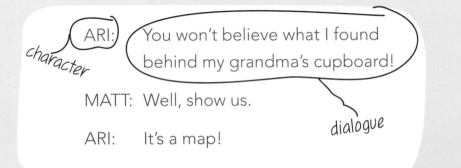

ARI: You won't believe what I found behind my grandma's cupboard!

character

MATT: Well, show us.

ARI: It's a map!

dialogue

Most plays start with a script.

In addition to dialogue, you will find **stage directions** in a play script. These are instructions that tell the actors how their characters should speak or behave. Like all instructions, stage directions are simple, clear, and direct so that they can tell the actor what to do quickly. To stop the actors from getting stage directions confused with dialogue, they are usually written in italics and inside parentheses (*like this*). For example:

JANA: (*excitedly*) What kind of map is it, Ari?

ARI: (*holding up the map*) Well, I recognize some of the places on it. And I think it might lead us to something interesting.

stage direction

MATT: (*whispers*) Like treasure?

The story in a play is shown through the actors' words and behavior. The audience isn't told about the characters' personalities or how they are feeling, but this information should be made clear through the way the actors perform.

Writing Tip

Some playwrights don't like to include many stage directions in their scripts. Instead, they leave the story for the director and actors to tell in their own way. Other playwrights include lots of stage directions, to make sure a complicated story is performed in a certain way. Plays based on adventure stories often include lots of stage directions, since they are full of action and it is important that the actors don't just move around randomly.

WHAT MAKES AN ADVENTURE PLAY?

Adventure stories make exciting plays! An adventure story usually involves a brave hero. He or she has to go on a quest to find something or save someone. This hero usually has to face challenges along the way and will reach a **low point,** where it seems that he or she will never win.

There will often be a villain who will try to stop the hero from reaching his or her goal. Usually, the hero wins in the end and the villain gets into trouble, so the play has a happy ending. Often the hero learns from his or her experiences over the course of the story.

Many adventure plays are based on adventure stories written by novelists. For example, the classic adventure story *Treasure Island* by Robert Louis Stevenson has been made into a play. It is the perfect adventure story, with the hero traveling on a ship, searching for treasure, and meeting pirates!

Like many adventures, *Treasure Island* is full of danger and narrow escapes!

The Lion, The Witch, and the Wardrobe is full of adventure and excitement.

Keeping things exciting

In an adventure play, there is always lots of danger and excitement. To make the story a gripping one, there is fast-paced action, and the characters have experiences that are very different than the audience's everyday lives. In this type of play, there is often treasure to be found or a mystery to solve.

Usually, an adventure play takes place in an exotic or spooky setting, with fast dialogue that keeps audiences on the edge of their seats! Many such stories involve magic or travel. Adventure stories are often made into movies (such as in the picture above) because they are so fast-moving, but watching a live performance of a play adds an extra level of **suspense** and excitement.

Ideas for an adventure play

If you want to write an adventure play, start by thinking about other adventure stories you have read or seen in movies or other plays. You could even watch a movie version of a play. Think about the story and take notes. What are the main events, and who are the key characters? What can you leave out to make your play easier to stage?

You could use a **narrator** to help you tell the story. A narrator can explain parts of the story that you can't perform onstage. This may help fill long sections in the original story that you want to leave out of the play—perhaps because they involve many different scene changes.

The novel *The Lion, the Witch, and the Wardrobe* by C. S. Lewis has been written and staged as a play. The story is full of magic and wonder, which helps to keep the audience surprised and adds color and excitement to the play's **plot**.

The characters in *The Lion, the Witch, and the Wardrobe* include mythical creatures, talking animals, and a cruel witch.

The Treasure Seekers story map

You could create your own adventure story for your play. Think about the key elements in an adventure story and how you could build these into your play. It's useful to write your idea as a story before you turn it into a play. This will help you develop and improve your ideas. You may decide to add or leave out parts when you write the script. For example:

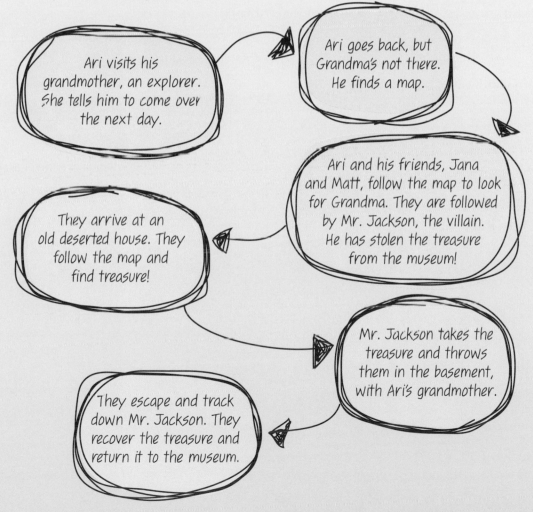

Ari visits his grandmother, an explorer. She tells him to come over the next day.

Ari goes back, but Grandma's not there. He finds a map.

Ari and his friends, Jana and Matt, follow the map to look for Grandma. They are followed by Mr. Jackson, the villain. He has stolen the treasure from the museum!

They arrive at an old deserted house. They follow the map and find treasure!

Mr. Jackson takes the treasure and throws them in the basement, with Ari's grandmother.

They escape and track down Mr. Jackson. They recover the treasure and return it to the museum.

Philip Pullman's *His Dark Materials* has been made into plays and a movie.

Characters in an adventure play

When your play begins, the audience knows very little about your characters. You need to introduce them—especially the main character—and show what's important about them early on in the story. The audience needs to know who the hero is and **empathize** with him or her as soon as possible.

Think about what clues you can give to help the audience understand the characters, from the way they talk, the clothes they wear, or the way they move. For example, you could get the villain to sneak around the stage silently all the time, so the other characters don't know he or she is there. You could also make the villain speak mysteriously or frequently lie to other characters. A hero will often have lots of energy and might run around the stage to show this. Try to build lots of these clues into your stage directions, to help the audience understand each character.

Typical characteristics of an adventure hero:
- Strong and brave
- Likes helping others
- Curious and gets into scrapes
- Smart enough to solve problems and riddles along the way
- A good leader with faithful friends.

Character notes from *The Treasure Seekers*

Make a list of all the characters in your play and write down what is important about each of them, what matters to them most, and how can you show this to the audience. For example:

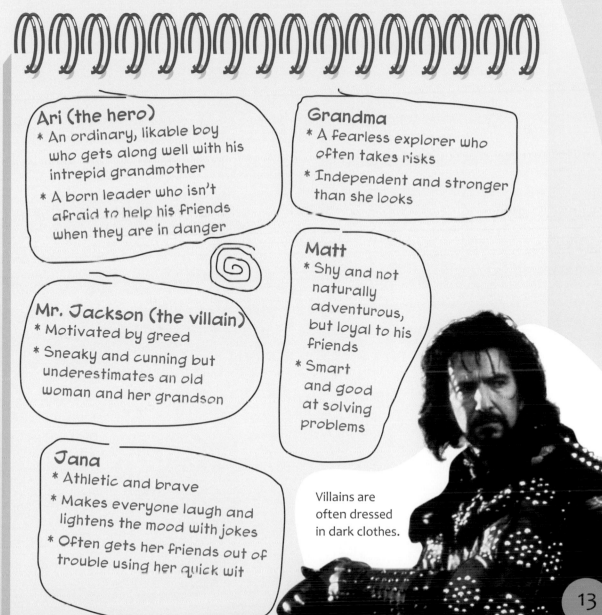

Ari (the hero)
* An ordinary, likable boy who gets along well with his intrepid grandmother
* A born leader who isn't afraid to help his friends when they are in danger

Grandma
* A fearless explorer who often takes risks
* Independent and stronger than she looks

Mr. Jackson (the villain)
* Motivated by greed
* Sneaky and cunning but underestimates an old woman and her grandson

Matt
* Shy and not naturally adventurous, but loyal to his friends
* Smart and good at solving problems

Jana
* Athletic and brave
* Makes everyone laugh and lightens the mood with jokes
* Often gets her friends out of trouble using her quick wit

Villains are often dressed in dark clothes.

WRITING AN ADVENTURE PLAY

Once you have your story map and characters figured out, you need to think about the details of your play and start writing!

Start with the plot

The plot of a play is the sequence of events that make up the story. Every scene in your play needs to show an important moment. Don't include any action or dialogue that isn't necessary or that might slow down the **pace**. An adventure story should be exciting and gripping! You can move forward in time with scene changes or take the action to a completely different place to keep things moving. A narrator could be used to explain any gaps in the story for the audience.

Your play will probably only have one main plot, but professional playwrights often include **subplots** in their work. These are parts of the story that move away from the main plot before coming together again at the end. They might tell a story of the minor characters or help underline the main message of the play.

A narrator can be like a storyteller on the stage, helping to move the action along.

The Glass Menagerie by Tennessee Williams uses memory and the past in interesting ways.

Flashbacks in *The Treasure Seekers*

Think about how you can move scenes forward or backward in time to keep things interesting. You could have a **flashback** scene, where a character remembers something in the past. For example:

ARI: How did you end up as an explorer, Grandma?

GRANDMA: It started when I was just a young girl…

(spotlight on actor playing part of Grandma as a young girl)

YOUNG GRANDMA: This book about the Amazon River is fascinating. But there's so much on the map left to explore. Why hasn't anyone written about that? I might just have to go there myself…

(lights back on Ari and Grandma)

GRANDMA: I was too curious. I wanted to find out more about the world.

Pace and tension

When you watch an adventure play, the action should keep you on the edge of your seat. The play should move quickly from one dramatic event to the next. It's important to keep up the pace throughout the whole performance. You don't want the story to get too slow or the audience to become bored.

When you write your script, make sure that the pace is fast enough and you don't dwell on one scene for too long. If you read your script aloud, it will be clear if you have any slow moments.

Try to keep your audience interested.

Try to build tension as you write your play. It should start with a relaxed feel. Soon, the audience should start to feel more suspense as you put obstacles in your hero's path. These setbacks should build up to the **climax** of the play—when the hero is in trouble and it looks like there's no way out. From here, you can move to the hero overcoming the problem and the story's **resolution**. There should be a release of tension at the end, when all the hero's troubles are sorted out and there is a happy ending. However, you could add a final **twist** to get everyone in the audience on the edge of their seats again!

Writing Tip

Sometimes the excitement and tension in a play can be too much for the audience! To help people relax for a moment, you can use **comic relief.** This means making people laugh and giving them a break from being on the edge of their seats.

Highs and lows

Check the pace and tension in your play by thinking about the highs (when tension is high) and lows (when the audience can relax a little) in your play. For example:

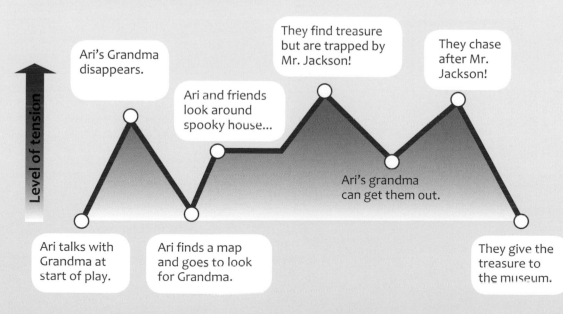

Level of tension

Ari's Grandma disappears.

Ari and friends look around spooky house...

They find treasure but are trapped by Mr. Jackson!

They chase after Mr. Jackson!

Ari's grandma can get them out.

Ari talks with Grandma at start of play.

Ari finds a map and goes to look for Grandma.

They give the treasure to the museum.

Writing dialogue

When you write the dialogue in your script, think about how language can be used in an adventure story to create tension and excitement. For example:

- You will often find short sentences that are used to build up suspense in a moment of danger. You can give your characters short, sharp bursts of dialogue to do this. You could use punctuation to do this.

- Contrast exciting moments with longer conversations during the more relaxed moments in the play. In moments of tension, you could add stage directions so the actors know to whisper, hiss, or shout.

Also think about how you can use dialogue to show the differences between your characters. Your adventure hero is probably a character who uses a lot of active language, such as "Let's go!," while other characters may be more thoughtful and cautious. Think about how you can use language to show the villain's character. You might want him or her to speak with harsh **alliteration**. For example, "Don't dare to defy me!" You could give characters interesting names to reflect their character—for example, "Professor Eville" if someone is the play's villain.

The way characters speak tells us about their personality.

When a character speaks directly to an audience, it changes the atmosphere onstage.

Writing Tip

Some playwrights, such as William Shakespeare, use **soliloquies** in their plays. This is when a character talks to him- or herself, sharing his or her thoughts with the audience. You could use this technique with the villain or hero in your adventure play, so the audience knows what this character is thinking and feeling.

Dialogue in *The Treasure Seekers*

Here is an example of how dialogue can be used to show character and create tension in *The Treasure Seekers*:

ARI: This is it. Let's go in!

MATT: *(nervously)* I don't know about this, Ari. We don't know what's in there—what if we get into trouble?

JANA: *(laughing)* I don't think anyone actually lives in a place like this!

ARI: We have to go in. Look—there's an open window we can climb through.

(They climb into the house.)

ARI: Okay, let's split up. I'll look upstairs.

GETTING STARTED

Once your play is written, you will want to get a team together to start **rehearsing**, or practicing staging, the play.

The director's role

You need someone to be in charge, and this person is the play's director. The director needs to have a vision of how the play will look and sound when it's finished. This person needs to be a good leader and be skilled at communicating with the other members of the team so that everyone knows what they need to do. It's a good idea for the director to have some experience with reading, acting in, and watching plays. He or she needs this knowledge to understand what will work well onstage. The director also needs to be a good listener, since other team members will have good ideas to share about how the play could be staged.

Marianne Elliott (right) is a well-known theater director. She directed *The Curious Incident of the Dog in the Night-Time.*

All good stories, including those we watch in the theater or movie theater, should keep us gripped.

Directing *The Treasure Seekers*

If you are directing a play like *The Treasure Seekers*, you may find the following suggestions helpful for your job:

1. Get to know the script well. Does the play remind you of any books or movies? If it does, spend some time re-reading those books or watching those movies to build up the world of the play in your mind.

2. Think about the characters and the sorts of actors you would like to play each **part**. Make some notes about the qualities that each character needs to display.

3. How could you create a set for the play? The scenes take place in Grandma's house, in the spooky house, and at the museum. Think about how you could show these different places in a simple way.

4. Finally, hold **auditions**. This is where people who want to act in the play can try out for various parts. When the actors read from the script, you can decide who will be best for each part. Now you have a **cast**!

Editing and rewriting your script

Once you've cast your play and the actors start to read their parts together, you may find that some parts of the play need to be reworked. Maybe some of the dialogue doesn't sound natural when the actors speak it. The actors might suggest lines that make more sense phrased another way. Ask the actors to question anything they feel isn't quite right.

Also, when you hear the play read aloud, you might find that some parts of the story are confusing or need more explanation. It's normal to realize there are issues like this only after the actors start asking questions about the script. Make note of these issues and make revisions to the play in these early stages.

It's important to read the script aloud together to see if you need to make any changes.

Checklist for revising and editing an adventure script

1 Listen to the actors read the whole script. Do any sections seem slow or boring? Is there any dialogue that doesn't help with explaining a character or moving the plot forward? Don't be afraid to cut anything that might slow the pace.

2 Is everyone clear on what each character wants to achieve in the story? If not, think about how you could edit the script to make things clearer for both the actors and the audience.

3 Ask your actors if they were surprised by any twists in your story. If they weren't, could you make these twists more unexpected and exciting?

4 Are there enough moments of tension in the play? Are the peaks in the action balanced with more relaxed moments when the audience can breathe again? Make sure there isn't too much or too little tension.

5 Listen to the dialogue. Does it sound natural? If something sounds odd, talk to the actors to find out how it can be improved.

Make sure to edit your play.

ACTING IN AN ADVENTURE PLAY

As you start rehearsing, everyone involved in the play needs to read and understand the whole script. Talk to the actors about their characters' motivation. You could put together a fact file about each character so each actor can remember the background and personality of his or her character.

Getting to know a character

You might like to play some **improvisation** games to explore the characters in your play. Actors don't use a script when they improvise. Instead, they think and speak as their characters, making up their lines as they go along.

For example, they could pretend to be in a certain situation and explore what their characters would do and say. Afterward they can talk about how they felt as they did this. Improvisation helps everyone to get a feel for the play's characters.

Getting to know your character might surprise you.

"The Interview Game"

Try playing this improvisation game to explore the characters in an adventure play:

1. Each actor thinks about his or her character: what is it about that particular character that makes him or her the most useful in the adventure? For example, how do the hero's skills and personality help when there are obstacles and setbacks to overcome? What useful experience does a character have to help in an adventure?

2. The rest of the team then fires questions at one actor at a time to decide who is the most useful in the adventure. The actors have to answer in character, as quickly as possible.

It is good practice to use improvisation to help your performance.

THEATER JOB

When a play is staged, it's often a good idea to have an **understudy** for each of the main parts. An understudy learns the lines of an important character in case the actor playing that part can't perform it. The understudy then steps into that **role** and the play can go ahead.

It is much better to perform in front of an audience when you are well-prepared.

Why do you need to rehearse?

You will need to rehearse your play before you perform it in front of an audience. As the director, you should create a rehearsal timetable for the whole team. Under each rehearsal date, write the names of the people who need to be there, so that they can easily see when they are needed. Tell your actors to let you know as soon as possible if they can't make a rehearsal, so you can rearrange if necessary.

Rehearsals usually begin with the actors just reading through the script together, but soon they start to act out each scene. The actors need to rehearse to learn how to speak and move. Once they have learned their lines, they will no longer need their scripts. Rehearsals are also important for the people working backstage to make sure everything runs smoothly.

TRY IT

Make sure your actors remember to face the audience when they speak; otherwise it will be very hard for the audience to hear them. Also remind your actors to concentrate when they are offstage. They need to listen to the **cues** so they know when to go back onstage.

In an adventure play, there will normally be lots of action sequences and dangerous moments. These scenes need extra practice, as the actors must know where they should stand at each moment and get their timing right. If the actors are unsure of things, the scene won't work, and any dramatic tension will be lost for the audience. Sometimes all this action can make a scene seem chaotic. However, if people practice, they will figure out the best way to move around the stage and speak at the same time!

As the director, you also have to be able to comment on your actors' performances. Any feedback you give isn't meant to be a **criticism** of their acting—it helps everyone to improve and perform better.

William Shakespeare's *Henry V* is full of action and danger.

BEHIND THE SCENES

Most plays have what is called a set. This is the **backdrop** to the scenes of the play and shows the location where the action takes place. In professional theaters, the sets for adventure plays can be huge and complicated. They can have lots of moving parts and special effects. For school plays or performances just for fun, it will be fine to create simpler sets.

Ideas for a simple but effective backdrop

To create a simple backdrop, you could paint large pieces of cardboard or just put up curtains. You could paint a scene on a large piece of paper and hang it up at the back of the stage. It's quick and easy to change this for another sheet of painted paper when you change scene. Keeping things simple will add to the mystery of your play's setting.

THEATER JOB

A set designer works with the director in a theater to design and build the sets for a play. He or she makes sketches after reading the play and watching rehearsals and then builds models to show how the sets would work. He or she works with **carpenters**, sculptors, painters, and other craftspeople to build and maintain the sets.

Set designers have to draw detailed plans for their design ideas.

Some sets are very complicated and need many people to build them.

Set ideas for *The Treasure Seekers*

Adventure plays often involve characters in unusual and dangerous situations. It's helpful if the set creates an exciting atmosphere. Here are some ideas for the scenery in *The Treasure Seekers*:

Grandma's house
* Colorful curtains to create the look of a friendly home
* Paint some statues on cardboard and hang up maps and photographs of faraway locations to show Grandma's past as an explorer
* A large cupboard where Ari finds the secret map

The spooky house
* Black curtains (at the back of the stage) to make this a dark and scary place

The museum
* Simple, brightly lit background to show this is a safe place
* Paint artifacts on cardboard or paper and hang them up

Costumes

Look for costumes for your play as early as possible. Start by thinking about the time and setting of your play. Should the actors wear ordinary, everyday clothes they already own, or do they need historic or traditional costumes?

If the play is set in another time period, you may need to look in books or on the Internet to see what sort of clothing was worn then. If your adventure play features characters such as pirates, you may be able to find suitable costumes in your local costume store.

If your play is set in the present, it will be easier to find costumes. However, check if you need any special clothes, such as a business suit or a police uniform. Give yourselves more time to find or make these more complicated costumes first.

Costume designers in theaters spend a lot of time looking at clothes worn by people in the past.

30

Try to rent historical costumes if you need them, since they will be difficult to make.

Remember to keep the items of clothing required to a minimum. For example, an actor playing a policeman may only need to wear a policeman's hat for the audience to realize what he is.

Costumes in *The Treasure Seekers*

Here are some ideas for costumes for the characters in *The Treasure Seekers*:

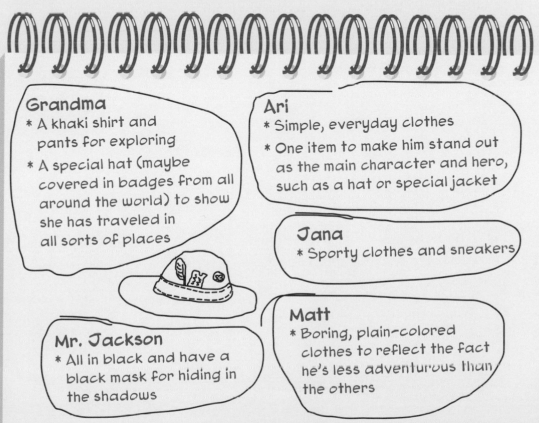

Grandma
* A khaki shirt and pants for exploring
* A special hat (maybe covered in badges from all around the world) to show she has traveled in all sorts of places

Ari
* Simple, everyday clothes
* One item to make him stand out as the main character and hero, such as a hat or special jacket

Jana
* Sporty clothes and sneakers

Mr. Jackson
* All in black and have a black mask for hiding in the shadows

Matt
* Boring, plain-colored clothes to reflect the fact he's less adventurous than the others

31

Props

The word *props* is short for "properties." It means any object that appears on the stage that isn't scenery or part of a costume. It is important to put one person in charge of props, as the props manager. He or she should know where every prop is at all times. Props need to be where the actors can find them at the right moment.

Props should be small or light enough to be carried onstage by the actors. In an adventure play, they may include explorer's equipment, such as ropes, maps, and backpacks. Other adventure stories may use exciting or dangerous-looking objects, such as treasure, ancient artifacts, or swords. Most of these things can be easily made from cardboard or papier maché, or you could buy them cheaply in thrift stores or toy stores.

This prop designer is making a gorilla for a play.

Staining paper with tea makes it look aged and creates a perfect prop!

Props for *The Treasure Seekers*

Here are some props you could include in *The Treasure Seekers*, with ideas about how to find or make them:

- *The map Ari finds*: You can make this yourself. Stain a piece of paper with cold tea and crumple it up to make it look older.

- *Artifacts in Grandma's home*: Make these out of papier maché or find some unusual objects in thrift stores.

- *Flashlights for exploring the spooky house*: These should be easy to borrow from friends and family.

- *Treasure chest filled with treasure*: You might be able to find toy treasure or cheap costume jewelry in a thrift store. If you can't borrow a small chest, you could make one by painting a cardboard box with a lid.

Lighting and sound

A lot of the excitement and tension in an adventure play can be created using light and sound effects. When you stage a play, it's usual to have people in charge of the lighting and sound. These technicians have to sit through the entire play, concentrating hard. They need to know exactly when to change what can be seen or heard onstage.

The lighting technician will start work with the director when rehearsals begin, to discuss how lights can be used in the play. Lighting can be quite dramatic in an adventure play. Effects could include flashing lights or color filters that create different moods and suggest different times of day. You could also use spotlights that highlight the character who is speaking. If the stage suddenly goes dark, this can surprise and shock the audience.

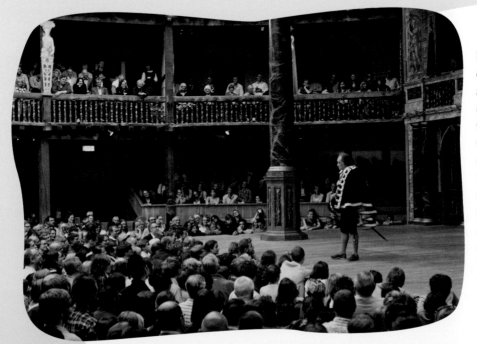

Hundreds of years ago, before electricity, theaters were usually outdoors. Plays had to be performed in the daylight, like this one at the Globe Theater in London.

Professional theaters use a sound system to control volume and quality of sound from microphones and speakers.

Sound can be equally as effective in building tension and adding to the thrill of action sequences. Fast music can make a situation feel more urgent or dangerous, and certain sounds can create a spooky feeling. Many professional theaters have orchestras playing live music during performances. They can play music from a **score** and make dramatic sound effects using their instruments.

Other theaters use recorded music during plays. It's important to remember that you have to pay a fee to use music that is in **copyright**. To avoid this, you could ask friends who play instruments to compose their own music or create their own sound effects for you.

People have performed plays for thousands of years, long before electrical lighting was invented. The first theaters were built in the open air so that sunlight would hit the stage when the actors performed. Later, some theaters used candles to help light up the stage. In the 17th century, many playhouses in Europe had chandeliers containing candles hanging from the ceiling. Unfortunately, they kept dripping hot wax onto the audience!

CREATING ATMOSPHERE IN YOUR ADVENTURE PLAY

When you stage your adventure play, you will want to create as much excitement and tension as possible. There are many ways to appeal to audiences' different senses.

Getting the sounds right

Think about what sound effects you can use to keep audiences on the edge of their seats. Watch adventure movies to get ideas. You could bang a drum slowly to build up to a dramatic moment, or scrape a bow on violin strings to make everyone nervous!

Animal noises will make the audience believe they are in another place. For example, use parrots and monkey sounds for a jungle scene or seagulls for a desert island. An owl hooting or bats screeching at night can help create a spooky mood. Use the Internet to find out how these animals sound, then either record their sounds or practice making noises like them. You can also get someone to make these sounds offstage during performances.

Experiment with drums to make some atmospheric sounds.

Play around with the lights to see what effects you can make using shadow.

Playing with light and shadows

When you plan the lighting for your play, also think about the effects caused by shadows and darkness. When your characters find themselves in danger, you might want areas of the stage to be dark, to create a more threatening atmosphere. If you are working with very simple lighting, you could give your actors flashlights to create a dramatic effect as they move around on a dimly lit stage.

Creating your own fog

See if you can borrow a fog machine, and ask an adult to help you use it for scenes where characters are lost or entering a strange and dangerous place. The machine produces a harmless **vapor** that looks like fog. It can leave the audience wondering what might be lurking in the shadows.

ALMOST THERE

A play doesn't work without an audience. Just as a book needs people to read it, you need people to come and watch your performances. You will need to **promote** your play to spread the word and get people interested in coming.

Attracting attention for your play

You could start by thinking about who might be interested in an adventure play. Find out if any classes at your school are studying adventure stories and let their teachers know about your play. You could also talk to your school or local librarian. See if they can let people who enjoy reading adventure fiction know about your play.

Make posters or **fliers** to advertise your play. You can give them to teachers and librarians to put on bulletin boards or you can hand them out at school. It is a good idea to include some images of the actors in their costumes on the fliers. Choose a dramatic scene, to show how exciting your adventure play will be.

Take a look at theater posters for famous shows to get ideas for your own poster.

Treasure Seekers

Directed by Mary Wilson

A thrilling story of adventure, risk, and discovery!

STARRING

BILL WHITE as Arl

RACHAEL SIM as Jana

JANE ROBERTS as Grandma

Wednesday, March 4—Saturday, March 7, at 8 p.m. at The Theater, Hill School

E-mail the main office

— title of play

— director

— people playing the main characters

— where and when the performance is

— how you get tickets

Spread the word widely! You could put an announcement about the play in your school newsletter, community web site, or local newspaper. Some local radio shows will read announcements about what's going on in the local community; if you contact them, they may even interview you about the play!

Don't forget the word-of-mouth method! Tell all your friends and family about the play. Ask them to speak to other people they know about it, too.

TRY IT

Professional theaters and amateur productions use **social media** to promote a new play. They put photos or articles about the play online, on places such as Facebook and Twitter. This lets them reach a potential audience for free. People who like the sound of the play can then easily share this information with their friends and followers, at the click of a button!

Ready for the show

As the day of your first performance gets closer, you will need to start getting everything ready. This means making sure that all the costumes are finished and fit the actors, that all the props are ready, and that any problems are fixed. It's a good idea to make front- and backstage checklists to make sure everything is where it should be and that nothing is lost or misplaced.

There is still time to give your actors last-minute tips!

Sometimes actors may get nervous toward the end of their rehearsals. It's important that nobody gets too stressed out. Remember that you are staging this play for fun. You all want to do your best, but you should also relax and enjoy yourselves! Go through the final rehearsals and preparations carefully and focus on any scenes that need extra work. Make sure everyone has rested before the performances start.

Many members of the audience will want to read a program to find out more about the play.

You will also need to organize ticket sales and seating for your audience. Make **programs** for the play, listing the names of all the actors and their characters, as well as the names and jobs of the backstage **crew**. You could include a short **synopsis** of the play in the program. Find some people to help you out with **front-of-house** work, such as selling tickets and handing out programs.

Previews

Professional theaters often have preview performances before a show officially opens, where a group of people are invited to watch and comment on the play. Their feedback helps the director, actors, and the crew to identify and correct problems. The opening night is attended by theater critics who will watch the play and write reviews for newspapers or magazines. Perhaps you can invite some friends to watch your play before it opens and ask them for feedback.

GO FOR IT!

The day is finally here—you are going to perform your play for the first time! Remind yourselves how hard you have all worked to get to this point. Putting on a play is a tremendous team effort and can take weeks of preparation. Now you can finally bring it to life and share your work with an audience!

Try not to worry about what might go wrong. You can set your mind at rest by being as organized as possible. Do some last-minute checks to make sure the costumes and props are all where they should be and nothing is missing. Run through the lighting and sound cues with the technical crew one last time to check that everyone knows what to do.

The actors should know when to arrive for the performance. If they come too early, they will be hanging around and getting nervous, but if they arrive too late, then everyone will be in a rush and a panic. There should be just enough time to put on costumes and makeup and do a few warm-up exercises. Then, take a few deep breaths and get ready to start.

Before the play starts, make sure everything is working.

Enjoy the performance of your finished play.

After the performance, take time to listen to the audience's **applause** and take your bows. It's important to enjoy this moment! Don't let your actors rush off at the end of the show, though. Make sure they give their costumes back to the costume manager and return any props they used to the correct place, so that everything is ready for the next performance.

Hopefully writing and staging an adventure play has been a fun adventure for you, too! Maybe you now have a new idea for a play you can't wait to write down...?

The Romans made applause popular. It used to be that soldiers clapped as a way to scare their enemies, but eventually people used applause in the theater to show appreciation.

GLOSSARY

alliteration effect when words begin with the same sound

applause show approval by clapping

audition test for actors to try out for particular roles

backdrop background to a set

carpenter person who makes things out of wood

cast give actors roles in a play; the collective name for all the actors in a play

climax most intense part of a story or play

comic relief moment when the audience laughs and tension is broken

copyright legal right to use a piece of music, writing, or art

crew people working backstage on a play

criticism feedback

cue signal to an actor to move or speak

dialogue words actors speak

director person in charge of staging a play

empathize understand the feelings of others

flashback scene that returns to earlier events

flier small leaflet giving information

front-of-house area of the theater business concerning the audience, such as ticket sales

improvisation sketch made up by actors as they go along

line sentence of dialogue in the script

low point hero's worst moment in the play

narrator person who describes and explains what is happening

pace moving at a steady speed

part role in a play

playwright person who writes the text of the play

plot story of a book, movie, or play

program booklet for audience members giving information about the play, cast, and crew

promote encourage people to like or do something

prop object that actors can move around onstage

rehearsing practicing acting in order to get ready for a performance

resolution moment where obstacles are overcome

role character or part in a play

score music written for a play or movie

script text of the play

set scenery and furniture on the stage

social media web sites where people can share ideas and information

soliloquy speech where a character says his or her thoughts aloud to the audience, rather than to the other characters in the play

stage direction instruction for an actor in a script for a play

subplot less important part of the story

suspense feeling of excitement and anxiety

synopsis summary of a story

tension emotional strain and stress

twist unexpected change of direction in the plot

understudy person who learns another's role in order to act at short notice in case the other person is sick

vapor gas or small drops of liquid made from heating a liquid or solid

FIND OUT MORE

Web sites

FactHound offers a safe, fun way to find Internet sites related to this book. All of the sites on FactHound have been researched by our staff.

Here's all you do:

Visit www.facthound.com
Type in this code: 9781484627709

Most cities and many towns have theater companies that put on plays for kids. Do research to find the theaters near you that offer plays for kids or theater training for young people. Perhaps you could ask if you could visit and look around, or ask about plays that are coming up. Check to see if there are any workshops with the actors or the writers.

Plays to read

Jennings, Coleman A. *Theatre for Young Audiences: 20 Great Plays for Children.* New York: St Martin's Griffin, 2005.

McRory Martin, Justin. *12 Fabulously Funny Fairy Tale Plays.* New York: Teaching Resources, 2002.

Shephard, Aaron. *Stories on Stage.* Friday Harbor, WA: Shephard Publications, 2005.

You can also hink about some of your favorite classic adventure stories, such as *Jack and the Beanstalk* or *The Wizard of Oz*. With an adult's help, you can find different stage adaptations of these classics. If you visit your local library, you can also find new plays you haven't heard of before that are full of adventure.

Drama game

If you enjoyed the "The Interview Game" and the improvisation game where you got to know your character earlier in the book, perhaps try the following improvisation game, too.

"Standing Still"

This game is a perfect way to start any rehearsal. Everyone in the room should stand as still as they can in a circle. They should each watch the person to their right and copy that person If he or she moves. Even when people are trying to stay still, they still move a little bit! As an extension, watch the person two to the right of your neighbor. Another fun thing to do is to exaggerate any movement you see by 50 percent. This will make this movement bigger and bigger every time it reaches a new person!

INDEX